# VOLLEYBALL
## FITNESS AND TRAINING

ZACHARY A. KELLY

The Rourke Corporation, Inc.
Vero Beach, Florida 32964

PHOTO CREDITS:
All photos © Tony Gray

PROJECT EDITORIAL SERVICES:
David Jones, Connie Denaburg

EDITORIAL SERVICES:
Penworthy Learning Systems

**Library of Congress Cataloging-in-Publication Data**

Kelly, Zachary A., 1970-
    Volleyball—fitness and training / Zachary A. Kelly.
        p.  cm. — (Volleyball)
    Includes index.
    Summary: Concentrates on skillbuilding for the serious player, including basic warm-up and cool-down, offensive and defensive practice drills, and specific techniques for practice alone or with a partner.
    ISBN  0-86593-505-X
    1. Volleyball—Training—Juvenile literature. [1. Volleyball.]  I. Title  II. Series: Kelly, Zachary A.,  1970-  Volleyball.
    QV1015.5.T73K45  1998
    796.325—dc21                                                              98–8566
                                                                                        CIP
                                                                                        AC

**Printed in the USA**

# TABLE OF CONTENTS

# BASIC RUNNING DRILL

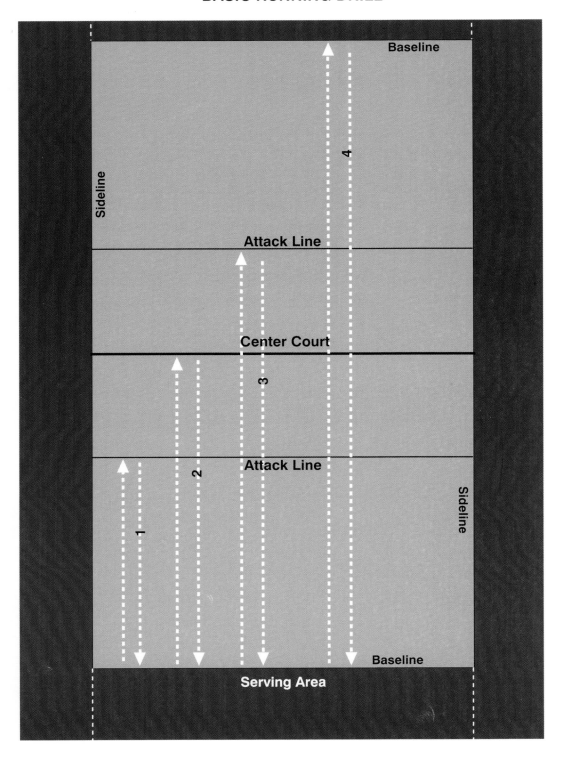

# PHYSICAL TRAINING

## Why Warm Up?

Volleyball is a fierce sport. Players jump, sprint, fall, hit, and move constantly. This kind of explosive movement demands a lot of your body and can hurt you. The best way to prevent injuries and improve your body's performance is through physical training.

The first step in physical training is warming up. A **warmup** raises your body's temperature by getting blood to your muscles. Muscles work better with more blood flowing through them. They tend to flex instead of being torn or pulled.

"Warm" muscles take the shock of a fall better than "cold" muscles, making impact easier on your joints. A good warmup makes you flexible and quick, letting you jump, land, or fall with greater power and fewer injuries. Good warmups include jogging, jumping jacks, or jumping rope for three to five minutes.

After you have warmed up, blood is flowing through your muscles, and your joints have been working a few minutes. Now you are ready to stretch.

## Stretching and Cooling Down

Stretching is a flexibility exercise for your muscles and joints. It helps increase the range of motion in your joints, which lets you bend farther and make complete movements. It also helps your muscles. Stretching helps your muscles to extend their full length; then, contract and relax more quickly. So stretching helps you move fast on the court and keeps you relaxed during play.

Many parts of your body need stretching, including your legs, back, shoulders, arms, and neck. Choose several stretches to focus on the main muscles you will be using.

★ **DID YOU KNOW?**

There are over 12,700 schools with 358,000 girls playing volleyball in the United States every year.

6

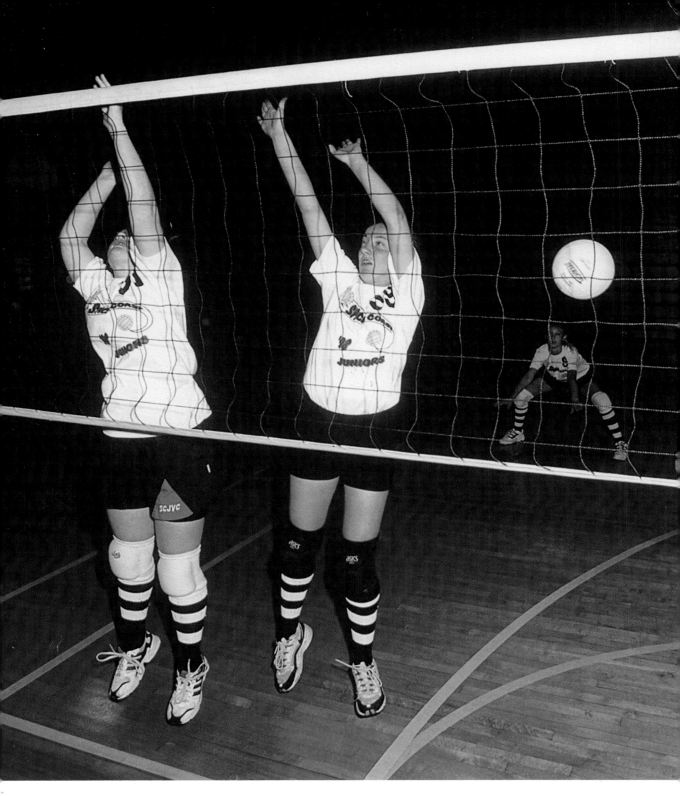

These players jump at the net to practice blocks.

You should stretch your muscles prior to every practice and game.

When you stretch, hold yourself in position for 7 to 12 seconds. Do not bounce. Bouncing tends to pull your muscles, not stretch them. Move slowly and gently into your stretch and out of it. Repeat each stretch two or three times.

At the end of a workout, take time to "**cool down**." Decrease your activity over a 5 minute period, then stretch again. Cooling down helps avoid stiffness and injury.

## Aerobics and Anaerobics

The body has two ways for turning the stored energy in the cells into muscle movement. Exercise that lasts for 3 minutes or more makes the body use oxygen to convert stored energy into action. These movements are called "**aerobic**." Aerobic movements are exercise like running, jogging, jumping rope, and swimming.

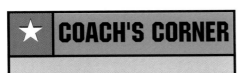

In emergency techniques, stay as close to the floor as possible before hitting the ball. This will help prevent injury.

Movements that last from 10 seconds to about 3 minutes are called "**anaerobic**." The body does not need oxygen to convert the cell energy into these motions. Instead the body uses chemicals found in the muscles to convert the energy. Anaerobic activities include short sprints, hitting an object, jumping up, and even spiking a volleyball.

To prepare the body for volleyball, practice both kinds of movement. Aerobic exercises increase endurance on the court. They strengthen the heart and lungs, giving you power that lasts over a long period without fatigue. Anaerobic activities help you move quickly and precisely.

All sports allow teams time to warmup prior to every game. Take advantage of this time and you can decrease the chance of injury to your body.

**Running is good aerobic exercise.**

Standing in one spot while tipping the ball will help you with ball control.

## Training for the Game

Physical training for volleyball includes warming up, stretching, cooling down, and aerobic and anaerobic exercise. Another part of physical training, called practice, teaches your body to perform in games.

Practice means doing over and over the actions you use in a game. When a muscle repeats a certain movement many times, it learns that movement. As they practice, players focus on *what* they do (certain moves), *how* they do it (form), or how *well* they do it (accuracy). If they have trained their muscles to perform well in practice, those muscles will perform well in a game. Whether practicing alone or with a team, make the practice as much like a game situation as possible. Focus on your form and accuracy for offense and defense techniques.

Off-court training is another way of keeping fit. Today, many coaches put their teams in weight rooms for basic weightlifting to help improve strength. Between games or during the off season, many players take up running to help keep them fit.

The next three chapters give you drills to practice serving, passing, and other moves. As you practice, keep trying to improve your skills. You will be training for the game.

# SERVING DRILLS

## The Toss

Several serves begin with the server tossing the ball into the air. This toss can make a good serve or a poor one. For overhand serves, the player tosses the ball 2 or 3 feet (over 1/2 meter or almost 1 meter) in the air. Try not to toss the ball too high and lose control.

The following three-step ball-toss drill will help you improve how you toss the ball. First, center a 12-inch (30-1/2 centimeters) sheet of paper in front of your forward foot.

Second, stand in serving position with your hitting hand fully extended. Third, toss the ball into the air so that it lands on the paper target. Practice the 2- or 3-foot (over 1/2 meter or almost 1 meter) toss of the **overhead floater**. Concentrate on the ball and keep your hitting arm in place. Your goal is to hit the target nine out of ten tosses.

## Over the Net

The serve-to-the-wall drill allows you to practice serving the ball above the net without thinking about distance. This drill has three steps.

First, place a strip of tape on the wall at net height. Second, stand about 20 feet (6 meters) from the wall in serving position. Third, serve to the wall, hitting the ball above the tape.

Begin with easier serves and change when you aim consistently. Your goal is to serve the ball above the tape nine out of ten times.

The next drill lets you move farther and farther from the net while practicing clean serves. This across-the-court drill has three steps.

★ **DID YOU KNOW?**

There are over 390,000 high school students who play for their schools annually.

Players line up to practice serves.

A topspin serve works well when the ball is tossed at the right height.

First, find a partner. Second, you and your partner stand on opposite sides of the net about 20 feet (6 meters) from it. Third, serve the ball without touching the net so that your partner can catch the ball without moving more than one step. Increase distance one foot at a time as you achieve consistency.

Focus on form (how you toss or move your hitting arm, for example.) Your goal is to serve eight out of ten "clean" serves.

## Distance and Accuracy

The corner-serve drill works on distance and accuracy. Use it to find out how much force and what angle are required to serve to the far corner. This corner-serve drill has three steps.

First, find a partner. Second, stand at opposite corners of the court. Third, serve the ball to your partner without touching the net.

Serving across the entire court takes a powerful hit. Your goal is to serve the ball properly nine out of ten times.

**★ COACH'S CORNER**

Stretching is a good way to prevent injury. Do it before and after playing.

The target-the-area drill helps you develop accuracy in serving to a particular area of the court. Accurate serving allows you to serve to weak areas of an opponent's court. The drill has three steps.

First, divide the court into six equal areas and number them from 1 to 6 in rotation order. Second, place a 10-foot (3-meter) square of paper on Area 1. Third, serve to that area of the court.

Your goal is to hit the papered area 5 times in fewer than 15 serves. Practice serving to each area (move the paper to Area 2 and so on).

**Practicing helps improve your overhand serve.**

# TARGET-THE-AREA DRILL

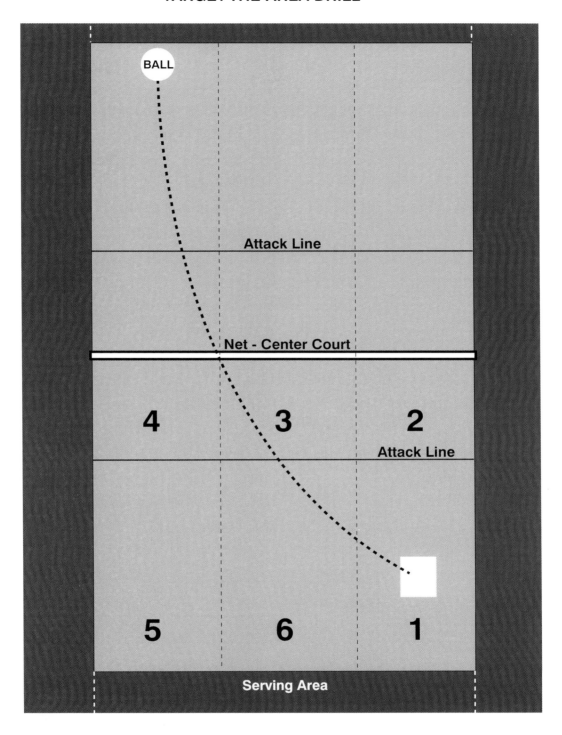

## For the Game

A drill named call-your-serve is similar to the target drill. It allows you to target the ball to a specific area of the court. This drill has three steps, too.

First, divide the court into six equal areas and number them 1 to 6 in rotational order. Second, your partner stands on the opposite side's serving area and calls a target number. Third, you serve into that target area.

This drill uses points to achieve your goal. Hitting the target area earns three points. Hitting an area next to your target earns two points. Hitting into any back court area earns one point. Your goal is 20 points in 10 serves.

The following drill lets you practice serving while others practice receiving. This call-the-pass drill has four steps.

First, find three other players to play on the opposite side as left back, right back, and right forward. Second, serve to the back of their court. Third, the left back or right back calls for the ball and receives it, sending it to the right forward. Fourth, the right forward tosses the ball back to the server.

The server's goal is 10 out of 12 clean serves. The back players' goal is 7 out of 12 good **forearm passes**.

# PASSING DRILLS

## Passing

Here are three good drills for improving your ability to pass the ball. The held-ball drill gives practice in forearm passing without moving to the ball. This drill has two steps.

First, have your partner hold the ball loosely toward you. Second, hit the ball over your partner's head with a forearm pass.

Keep your arms away from your body and parallel to your thighs. Your goal is 25 good forearm passes out of 30 tries.

The partner-toss drill allows you to hit a ball that's moving right at you. Use partner-toss to work on distance and height of your passes. This drill has two steps.

First, have your partner toss the ball to you. Second, use the forearm pass to hit the ball so that your partner can catch it without moving more than one step in any direction. Your goal is 20 good forearm passes in 25 attempts.

The bumping drill allows you to practice your passing form while moving. This drill has two steps.

First, toss the ball up and let it drop. Second, bump it net high repeatedly, staying within a 10-foot (3-meter) square. Your goal is 25 bumps in a row.

## Accuracy

A drill named pass-to-a-target lets you practice moving to the ball. This drill has four steps.

First, find two partners. Second, one player stands across the net as the tosser. Stand across from the tosser behind your attack line. The third player acts as your target on your side of the court. Third, the tosser tosses the ball to you. Fourth, you pass it to your target. Your goal is 20 successful forearm passes out of 25 tries.

**★ COACH'S CORNER**

If you have a hard time with a certain technique, do not give up. Ask your coach, ask your teammates, and practice it. Individual drills often make the difference between an intermediate player and an advanced player.

This player uses a forearm pass to practice bumping the ball.

These players practice forearm and overhead passes in front of the net.

The following move-and-pass drill provides a game situation: You will move as you pass the ball. This drill has five steps.

First, find two partners. Second, your partners stand 20 feet (6 meters) apart on your attack line. Face them while standing near your end line. Third, move in front of one player. Fourth, that player tosses the ball to you; and you pass it back 2 feet (about 1/2 meter) above net height so that he or she can catch it within one step. Fifth, move in front of the other player. Your goal is 20 accurate passes out of 25 attempts.

## Overhead Pass

With the pass-bounce-pass drill you can practice overhead passing without having to worry about the force of your pass. This three-step drill is useful for beginning players who are afraid of hurting their fingers.

First, pass the ball at least five feet (1-1/2 meters) into the air. Second, let it hit the floor. Third, as the ball rises, pass it again five feet up.

Stay within an area half the size of your side of the court. Your goal is 25 consecutive overhead passes.

★ **DID YOU KNOW?**

To improve quickly, play often with players more advanced than you.

The two-step overhead-toss-and-pass drill gives practice in hitting a ball coming into the high zone.

First, have a partner toss the ball easily toward you at or above your head. Second, use an **overhead pass** to return the ball so that your partner can catch it without moving more than one step in any direction. Your goal is nine good overhead passes to your partner out of ten tries.

**A team practices the triangle drill.**

These players show good technique in practicing the overhead pass.

## Overhead Accuracy

The triangle drill allows you to practice back passing and passing at various distances. This drill has four steps.

First, three players stand in a line about 10 feet (3 meters) apart. Two players should face one direction with the third player facing them. Second the player facing his or her partners begins with an overhead pass to the middle player. Third, the middle player sets the ball to the third player with a back overhead pass. Fourth, the last player passes the ball long to the first player.

Your goal is to complete all four steps 15 times without missing. When you reach the goal, rotate positions with the other players.

Another drill to practice back passing, as well as footwork and ball control, is called pass-move-pass.

First, two partners face each other on the court. Second, Player A overhead passes the ball to Player B and runs to a position behind Player B. Third, Player B receives the pass and back passes the ball to Player A. Then Player B turns to face Player A. Fourth, Player A passes the ball and begins the drill again. Your goal is 10 completions of steps 2-4.

## CHAPTER FOUR

# OFFENSE AND DEFENSE DRILLS

### Tips and Off-Speed Spikes

An offensive drill called tip-to-target gives you practice sending the ball to two weak areas of an opponent's court. This drill has four steps.

First, place two targets on the other side of the net—one 10 feet (3 meters) wide in the center front and one 5 feet (1-1/2 meters) wide opposite your left front. Second, one player stands at your right front position as the setter. You stand at the left front position as attacker.

A third player stands on a chair across the net from you as a blocker. Third, the setter tosses the ball high outside to you. Fourth, you tip the ball over the blocker's hands to either target. Your goal is five tips out of ten attempts in each target area.

The off-speed-spike drill allows you to practice sending the ball to another weak area of your opponent's court.

This drill is like the tip-to-target drill, except that the target is a 10-foot (3-meter) square centered on the attack line. Use an **off-speed spike** instead of a **tip** to hit it. Your goal is 10 off-speed spikes in the target area out of 15 attempts.

## The Spike

To practice your spiking form, use the wall-rebound drill. This drill has three steps.

First, stand 10 feet (3 meters) away from the wall. Second, **spike** the ball so that it lands about 5 feet (1-1/2 meters) from you. Third, when the ball rebounds off the wall, spike it again.

Concentrate on your form. Your goal is 25 spikes without missing.

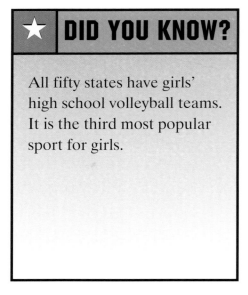

★ **DID YOU KNOW?**

All fifty states have girls' high school volleyball teams. It is the third most popular sport for girls.

A coach helps players practice a double block.

Learning to spike takes a lot of practice.

The spike-to-target drill also gives you practice in spiking the ball to weak areas. This drill has five steps.

First, place a 10-foot (3-meter) square target in both of your opponent's back corners. Second, stand in your left forward position and have a partner stand in the right forward position as setter. Third, pass the ball high to your partner. Fourth, your partner sets the ball to you. Fifth, without jumping, spike the ball into one of your target areas. Your goal is five hits out of ten in each target area.

## Digs

A drill named nonstop allows two players to practice digging with control and height. This drill has five steps.

First, Partner A tosses the ball and spikes it to Partner B. Second, Partner B **digs** the ball to partner A. Third, Partner A sets the ball to Partner B. Fourth, Partner B spikes the ball to Partner A. Fifth, Partner A digs the ball to Partner B and the drill goes on, nonstop.

This drill, commonly called pepper, allows both players to improve their digging. Your goal is five digs in one nonstop round.

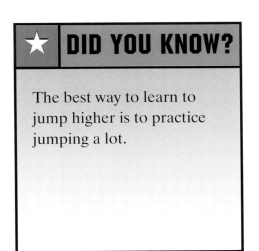

**★ DID YOU KNOW?**

The best way to learn to jump higher is to practice jumping a lot.

The back-court-digs drill prepares you for digging in any back court position. This drill has three steps.

First, your partner stands on a chair in the left forward position of your opponent's court. Second, your partner tosses and spikes the ball to you. Third, you dig the ball to center court at least 2 feet (about 1/2 meter) higher than the net.

Practice this drill in left back, center back, and right back position. Your goal is seven out of ten successful digs in each position.

**You have to be quick to hit a good dig.**

This player practices the dig-roll drill.

## Roll and Sprawl

The dig-roll drill focuses on your roll form without dealing with a hard spike. This drill has three steps.

First, stand in the left back position facing your partner, who stands near the net on your side. Second, your partner gently tosses a low ball to one side of you. Third, let the ball drop low; then dig it and **roll**, getting quickly to your feet. Your goal is five out of ten successful digs to either side.

The dig-sprawl drill is very similar to the dig-roll. In this drill, your partner tosses the ball so that it lands 3 or 4 feet (about a meter) in front of you. You dig and **sprawl**, getting to your feet quickly. Your goal in this drill is five successful digs out of ten.

When you reach your goal in the first two drills, have your partner begin spiking the ball at you. Decide for each spike whether you will roll or sprawl. Dig to the high center of your court. Your goal for this advanced drill, called dig-roll-sprawl, is seven out of ten attempts.

# RESOURCES AND ORGANIZATIONS

**Volleyball Information**

Millions of people all over the world play volleyball. Over 46 million Americans play the game regularly. Thousands of teams can be found in high schools and junior highs across the country. So how can you become involved? You can find information at a library or on the Internet.

Also, information may be found locally at the YMCA and YWCA, Boy's and Girl's Club, or a community volleyball league. A coach or physical education (PE) teacher at your school could likely tell you how to "get in the game."

School and public libraries usually carry several books about the sport. Some books offer playing tips along with rules of the game. The library also may have videos about volleyball. You can use a video to learn about the sport and to improve your form. Several sports magazines carry articles about volleyball, too. Other magazines, such as Volleyball USA, are devoted to this sport. A librarian will be able to help you find books, magazines, and videos.

Another place to get information about volleyball is your computer—if it has a CD-ROM drive and/or access to the Internet. Compact disks that teach about the sport are available in software stores. The Internet has excellent web sites that you can find by using the word "volleyball" to search.

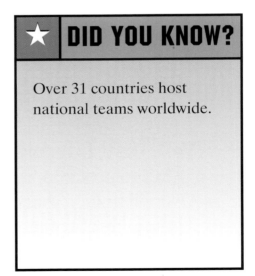

★ **DID YOU KNOW?**

Over 31 countries host national teams worldwide.

The hard work pays off during competition.

Joining a local volleyball league can be great fun.

## Want to Play?

Most high schools in the United States have at least one volleyball team. Junior high schools do not have teams as often as the high schools, but many do. If your school has a team, it might be the easiest way for you to begin playing. If not, you may want to find a team in your community.

Many communities have volleyball leagues. Businesses, churches, scouting groups, and other organizations sponsor teams. A team might practice once or twice a week and play against another team a few times a month. To find out about teams in your area, look in your local newspaper or talk with a coach or physical education teacher at school.

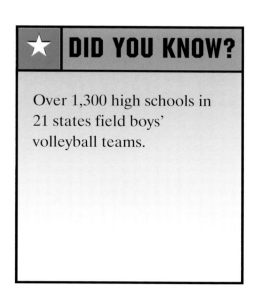

★ **DID YOU KNOW?**

Over 1,300 high schools in 21 states field boys' volleyball teams.

## Volleyball Organizations

Three large organizations promote the game of volleyball: the YMCA, the U.S. Youth Volleyball League (**USYVL**), and USA Volleyball (**USAV**). These organizations can help you.

At the YMCA (**Y**), you can join a team and begin playing. The Y has information about rules and helpful coaches for its teams.

The YMCA looks for experienced players to work as referees and coaches of beginner teams. Look in the telephone book for the location of YMCAs in your area. Call or go to one of them for answers to your volleyball questions.

The USYVL sponsors leagues for people ages 8 to 18 in major U.S. cities. The organization named USA Volleyball (USAV) controls volleyball in the United States. (In fact, the USYVL is part of the USAV.) This organization is a good source of information about professional leagues, major events, and other up-to-date facts. Its magazine, *Volleyball USA*, includes a telephone number that you can call for the USYVL team nearest you.

**With lots of hard work and practice, players can advance to the college level.**

A team pulls together during competition.

## Your Volleyball Coach

After you join a team, your coach will give you personal attention. The coach will note your strengths and weaknesses in the game. He or she will work with you to develop your weak areas and make you grow as a volleyball player. As you play, listen to your coach's comments. When your coach tells you what you do wrong or poorly, it is to help you play better.

Your coach will lead your physical training. He or she will give you drills to overcome weak points and make strong points even stronger. The coach will put you in a team with other players at your skill level.

Your coach likely could help you get more involved in the sport if you want to. Most coaches belong to organizations like USAV. Of all the ways you have to learn and play volleyball—from beginner to intermediate to advanced to Olympic teams—your coach is number one.

# GLOSSARY

**aerobic activity** (ai RO bik  ak TIV i tee) — continuous exercise such as cycling, jogging, or swimming, during which the muscles use mostly oxygen for energy

**anaerobic activity** (AN ai RO bik  ak TIV i tee) — short, intense activity during which the muscles use fuel other than oxygen for energy

**cool down** (KOOL  DOUN) — light exercise to stretch the muscles and slow the heart and respiration rates after intense exercise

**dig** (DIG ) — receiving an attack with a forearm pass, usually low in the back court

**forearm pass** (FAWR AHRM PAS) — the basic passing technique using the forearms as the contact area

**off-speed spike** (OFF-SPEED SPYK ) — rather slow, or less forceful spike; a "Dink" and "Tip"

**overhand floater** (O ver HAND  FLO ter) — a more advanced serve, performed with an overhand motion

**overhead pass** (O ver HAND PAS) — the basic passing technique using both hands and overhead motion

**roll** (ROL) — an emergency technique for receiving an out-of-range ball that involves rolling on the floor after contacting the ball

# GLOSSARY

**spike** (SPYK) — the attack move, performed by hitting the ball overhand over the net with a downward path

**sprawl** (SPRAWL) — an emergency technique for receiving an out-of-range ball that involves a low approach, forward on-the-floor motion, and landing on the chest

**tip** (TIP) — an off-speed attack; dink

**warmup** (WAWRM UP) — light exercise and stretching to increase blood flow to muscles and raise heart and respiration rates

# FURTHER READING

Find out more with these helpful books and information sites:

*American Coaching Effectiveness Program, Rookie Coaches Volleyball Guide.* Champagne, IL: Human Kinetics, 1993.

Howard, Robert E. *An Understanding of the Fundamental Techniques of Volleyball.* Needham Heights, MA: Allyn and Bacon, 1996.

Kluka, Darlene, and Dunn, Peter. *Volleyball.* Wm. C. Brown, 1996.

Neville, William S. *Coaching Volleyball Successfully.* New York: Leisure, 1990.

Vierra, Barbara, and Ferguson, Bonnie Jill. *Volleyball: Steps to Success.* Champagne, IL: Human Kinetics, 1996.


American Volleyball Coaches Association at http://www.volleyball.org/avca/index.html

Complete worldwide source for volleyball information at http://www.volleyball.org/
This site includes descriptions and ordering information for many new books and videos; also, many links.

Great links: http://users.aol.com/vballusa/index.htm

Online Volleyball Magazine subscription page at http://www.volleyballmag.com/sub.htm

More volleyball information at http://www.volleyball.com

# INDEX